HEARTS BURNING WITHIN US

ISBN 978-1-7333199-5-9
UPC 768413759365

Edited by Kathryn Siglow Kress.
Book design by Charis Publishing
Printed by Charis Publishing

Published July 2021

About the Authors

Anne DeSantis is the Director for the St. Raymond Nonnatus Foundation for Freedom, Family, and Faith headquartered in the Philadelphia area. She is married to her husband Angelo for over 30 years, with two adult daughters, and is a former homeschooling mother of 20 years. She is a 55+ model, actress, TV Host, and Co-Host of the Sewing Host Podcast with Bill Snyder. Learn more about her life and work at AnneDeSantis.com.

Maggie Riggins has served the Catholic Church in ministry with college students and young adults since 2001. Currently, she is the Director of the Office of Young Adult and Campus Evangelization in the Diocese of Allentown, PA. She is married to her husband Brett, and they have been blessed with a daughter, Raquelle.

Jennifer Southerton is the Campus Minister at Lourdes University, a small Catholic Franciscan school on the border of Michigan in Sylvania, Ohio. Jenn is a native of Lewisburg, Pennsylvania and an alumna of DeSales University, where she received her Bachelor's in Communication ('17), minored in Theology, studied abroad in Rome, and earned her Master's in Education ('19) while working as the Graduate Assistant for Campus Ministry. She is excited to become "Jennifer Okuley," as she marries the love of her life, Andy, this summer.

Bill Snyder is the Founder of Patchwork Heart Ministry, a non-profit Catholic Young Adult ministry. He inspires, engages, and challenges young people to live their faith boldly by example, through storytelling and various media initiatives. He is a member of the Council for Pentecost Today USA and serves as a Discerner for the Catholic Charismatic Renewal in the Archdiocese of Milwaukee. He and his wife Agnes were recently blessed with a baby boy, Elvin Francisco.

HEARTS BURNING WITHIN US

A collaborative work by:

Anne DeSantis
Magdalene Riggins
Jennifer Southerton
Bill Snyder

Preface

Several years ago, Bill Snyder, the founder of Patchwork Heart Ministry, conceived the idea for a Catholic question and answer book for college students. But soon after writing an introduction for the book it became an all-but-forgotten Google document. Until the worldwide Coronavirus Pandemic began...

The onset of the Coronavirus pandemic presented many challenges for humanity, society, and the Church. Widespread illness and unprecedented job loss locked down our society. Through the action and inspiration of the Holy Spirit, three Catholic non-profit ministries joined forces to bring light into darkness; Patchwork Heart Ministry, St. Raymond Nonnatus Foundation, and FIAT Ministry Network. Their collaboration inspired many new projects including, the Journeys in Faith TV Show, The Sewing Hope Podcast, and this book.

During a conversation Bill had with his Sewing Hope Podcast co-host, Anne DeSantis. He casually mentioned the idea for this book. Anne immediately breathed new life into the project inviting Magdalene Riggins to have a visioning conversation. A hop, skip, and a jump later we were joined by our fourth author, Jennifer Southerton along with five college students Adrian Anatalio, Veronica Gonzales, Jack Haase, Genevieve O'Connor, and Shawn DeSantis from Lourdes, DeSales, and Gwynedd-Mercy Universities. Meeting weekly via Zoom throughout the spring and summer of 2020 we spent time praying, asking, debating, and answering questions by having a dynamic and living conversation rooted in the truth and teachings of our Catholic Faith. This book is a result of that conversation.

As you will see in the pages that follow, these questions and responses are not just relevant, but rather they burn on the hearts of college-age young adults to be answered in truth and charity. They are not superficial.

It is with both gratitude for all those involved in the Spirit-led conversation, and with hope for all the hearts that will be set aflame by the Spirit through reading these pages that we present to you "Hearts Burning Within Us."

~ The Hearts Burning Within Us Team

Table of Contents

Questions 20-25 Living the Faith

Questions 26-34 Sharing the Faith

Questions 35-42 Growing in Faith

Introduction

At the end of the Gospel according to Luke, there is a story about two disciples of Jesus walking along a road to Emmaus who were rather confused at the events they had just witnessed. They had just seen an extraordinary man who had been preaching, inspiring, empowering and leading them for three years, die a criminal's death on a Roman instrument of torture and execution.

His message, while very countercultural, was a message of peace, justice, hope and life. He was certainly not a criminal in their minds. He was much more, for they believed and were hoping that He was going to "be the one to redeem Israel" (Lk 24:21) to use their words. But their hope had been defeated when He seemingly died three days earlier.

So far, does this sound anything like you? No, we don't mean physically walking along the dusty road to Emmaus, even we haven't done that. We mean feeling confused and defeated when it comes to understanding or being an active member of the Catholic Church.

Perhaps you've "tried" the Church in the past to help you deal with some of the issues and struggles in your life, and you left feeling more confused. Perhaps a friend or leader in the Church disappointed you or hurt you by not meeting your spiritual needs and desires or answering some of your tough questions, leaving you feeling defeated.

You've thought "The Church seemed like such a perfect place until THAT happened." Well then it looks to us like you've got quite a bit of stuff in common with our ancient friends at Emmaus. Let's go back to their story.

Now that they are utterly confused and disappointed, a mystery man joins them on their walk and starts asking them what they are talking about. Of course, they don't want to be rude, so they are polite and tell Him about that awful crucifixion a few days ago. To which He replies, *what crucifixion?*

They are shocked that He doesn't know what's going on – has He been living under a rock? (The answer is yes, but that is beside the point.) They ask Him, "are You the only visitor to Jerusalem Who does not know of the things that have taken place here these days?" (Lk 24:18)

They then tell Him all the details of the horrific events and finally, after they have poured out every last drop of drama and heartache from their devastating story, He says to them "Oh how foolish you are!" (Lk 24:25)

He then proceeds to tell them why they didn't understand what was really going on by explaining the meaning of the Scriptures, starting with Moses.

Again, you probably also have much in common with our biblical friends along this part of the path. Most people, when they are confused, like to find an answer so they tell others about their confusion and see if others can help them out.

You've likely told others about your confusion and struggles with your faith life. You've probably talked to your friends, parents, aunts and uncles, clergy, or even other adults you trust, searching for an answer.

The drama-saturated explanation of why your heart is unsettled and how your situation is different and why nobody else understands was told to these numerous people while you searched for an answer. At least one person listening to your story, has told you in some way "Oh how foolish you are," and given you a story or example from their life to show you that hope still exists.

Throughout the process of asking many people and receiving multiple responses you have found an answer. If this resonates with you, you have remained in stride with our friends along the road to Emmaus. But let's go back to their story one more time.

So now that these two disciples have received an answer to all their questions by this mystery man, they are very curious. They want to know who this guy is that has joined them on their journey. He says that his destination is not theirs and that He will be continuing further along the road.

But these two disciples beg and beg Him to stay overnight as they are both tired and hungry from their travels and he was probably as well. He agrees to stay, and they sit down for a meal. During that meal miracles abound. When He breaks the bread with them, their "eyes were opened, and they recognized" (Lk 24:31) that He was Jesus.

Then just as soon as they realize this, He disappears from their sight. All excited, they exclaim "Were not our hearts burning within us while He spoke to us on the way and opened the Scriptures to us." (Lk 24:32) and run to tell the other disciples and apostles hidden in the upper room about their encounter with Jesus.

Helping you recognize Jesus is where our book begins. Simply, we seek to dispel your confusion or that uneasy feeling of defeat by answering your questions. Maybe you have found some answers, but are looking for more (this book doesn't contain them all, nor does any book for that matter).

We will answer questions about faith, God and the Catholic Church and much like the last part of the story, we know with confidence that Christ will reveal himself, not through our answers but your experience of living the responses. Perhaps that is the most important thing to note: this book won't help you unless you give the Church a chance to reveal Christ to your heart.

In other words, if you don't attempt to practice the faith while you are reading this book by praying daily, attending Mass every Sunday and Holy Day of Obligation and celebrate the Sacrament of Reconciliation regularly, this book will be nothing more than a fun ride, (remember, that roller coasters might be fun, but they end at the same place they begin so you have gone nowhere in the end). Don't let that be you.

Nor is our book a magic trick to make Jesus appear or disappear (we can't do that no matter how hard we try), it is an instrument (we hope) that will draw you more closely into a relationship with Jesus Christ and His Holy Catholic Church and leave your hearts burning for more of Christ's love, a love that you will spread to the whole world.

Interpreting Scripture

1. *Since the Magisterium is made up of humans,
    who we know are fallible by nature, how can
    we know they are not, even if unintentionally,
    misguiding the community of faith with possible
    misinterpretations that may falsely claim to be
    guided by the Holy Spirit? What does the
    process look like of accepting dogma as
    dogma?*

A.   This question is foundational to answering all of
the remaining questions. First, let's define the
Magisterium. The Magisterium is the bishops in
communion with the successor of Peter (the Pope),
the Bishop of Rome (cf. CCC 85).[1] It is important to
understand this because, while the Pope is the one who
ultimately speaks with *Ex Cathedra* or "from the chair,"
the formal dogmas of the Church, the bishops also have a
role in helping define and pass on the faith to us the

----

[1] Catechism of the Catholic Church, Second Ed., USCC,
2019

faithful. When Jesus walked the earth, He taught *all* of the Apostles and shared His life with them intimately but left *one person* in charge in His absence to lead the apostles, St. Peter.

Likewise, today the Holy Spirit continues to guide the successors of apostles, the bishops, identically. The bishops all teach and pass on the faith to the faithful, but look to one leader among them, the Pope, for guidance, direction, and unity.

Now, to your question about the infallibility of this Magisterium. It can be confusing when, in both the long rich history of our faith and the recent past, there are a plethora of examples of the sins of bishops coming into the light of the public to believe that what this group of people teaches is perfect in the matters of faith and morals. Despite the best efforts of evil to infiltrate and influence the Magisterium of the Church and lead it and us, the faithful, away from the truth, the Church has remained true to the teachings of Christ. How do we know this to be the case?

The mere existence of the institution of the Church for over 2000 years is a good start. There is no other organization on the face of the earth, not even one, that has withstood the storms and scandals that the Catholic Church has withstood and still exists. The Catholic Church is the largest, most pervasive organization on the planet and feeds, clothes, provides shelter for, and educates more people than any organization in history.

This points to the fact that despite the ignorance and intentional sins of individuals within the hierarchy of the Church that the Church is not defined by their mistakes but the Holy Spirit. Simply, we know the truths the Catholic Church teaches to be authentic because they withstand the storms. It is just as Jesus says, "Heaven and earth will pass away, but my word will not pass away." (Matthew 24:34)

The teaching office of the Church, the Magisterium of the Church, is the agent the Holy Spirit uses to help us recognize what the enduring truths of our faith are in every age and season, and because of this "the gates of the netherworld shall not prevail against it." (cf. Matthew 16:18)

Finally, your question about what does accepting Dogma look like? I once heard a great quote during a talk by Catholic theologian and author Mark Shea about dogma that has stuck with me. He said, "dogma is the completion of a thought. It's almost like knowing 2+2=4. Once you know this you no longer need to think about it anymore."

The dogmas of the Church simply state we've thought about this, we know it to be true and you don't need to worry or waste your time thinking about it anymore – you can move on to other more pressing questions to think about.

They are often promulgated after long debates and discussions in which the Holy Spirit has revealed to the Church the truth and that it is necessary for us to build our faith upon. They are like having the essentials of a bat and ball to play baseball. We can discuss and debate a lot of other rules of the game, but without a bat and ball we can't even begin a game.

Incarnational Invitation

2.   *How can I keep the Lord's Day holy as a college student? Sunday is usually prime-time for cramming. Is that sinful?*

A.   I particularly like how this question is phrased. If I think about my college experience, I spent many Sunday's "cramming." However, more often than not, I made sure I attended Sunday Mass. My college (The University of Scranton) had two Sunday evening Masses one at 7 p.m. and another at 9 p.m. So even if I woke up a little later on Sunday morning, I could study in the afternoon and still make it to Mass on a Sunday night. (On some nights after Mass, I'd go back and cram more.)

With that being said, the Church teaches that we are obligated to attend Mass on Sundays (and Holy Days of Obligation) unless there is a grave reason why we cannot attend for not doing so. If a grave reason exists for you to miss Mass then the Church states that you should to "engage in prayer for an appropriate amount of time personally, as a family or in groups of families." (cf. CCC 2180-2183)

Therefore, you've got to decide a few things for yourself.

First, is "cramming" considered a serious reason to miss attending Mass? (Personally, I find it hard to make a case for that!) If so, is cramming more important than God? Did you try to spend an appropriate amount of time worshipping God? Or are you just going to say your schoolwork is more important than He is on Sunday and forget all about Him?

Some final food for thought: in the third commandment, God asks us to dedicate twenty-four out of one-hundred and sixty-eight hours in a week to stop our own work and worship Him. Most of us give Him a lot less (myself included). Intentionally cutting Him out of the picture so we can advance our studies, career, or enjoy a leisure activity while forgetting completely about Him is *definitely* sinful.

My suggestion to keeping the Sabbath day holy is to give God your best – at least on Sunday. What do I mean by that? Give Him the time when you are most attentive, awake, and alive.

Dedicate that to Him and worship Him. Attend Mass at that time, don't just squeeze Him in between homework assignments. Jesus doesn't tell you that He'll make some time for you right after He's done defeating Satan for the day, so likewise I wouldn't tell Him you only have got time for Him after studying for a midterm.

Response to Those
<u>Not Following "All the Rules"</u>

3.   *How should I respond when someone says
      they are not Christian/Catholic because of
      "all the rules?"*

A.   I'd ask them to which "rules" they were referring.
I don't mean to be blunt here, but I'd get specifics.
Oftentimes, people like to make up their own
interpretations of Church "rules."

    Don't let them be vague – ask them their objections
then you can begin to enter into a deeper conversation
about what the Church teaches and why.

    As a starting point, it might be helpful to draw an
analogy between playing a board game and the "game" of
life: without defined rules, a game has no set purpose or
objective. The "rules" of our faith act as guidelines that
define our purpose on earth and help us achieve the end
goal which is heaven.

It's especially important that as you have this conversation of drawing somebody in through their objections that you navigate it with gentleness, reverence, and respect. You don't have to know all the answers to respond to them in this way either. Just find out what they are referring to and then you can both do the research and grow in faith together.

Veneration – Not Worship – of Mary and the Saints

4. *How do you respond when someone asks if Catholics worship Mary and the saints?*

A. Catholics don't worship Mary or the saints. Saints are fallible people who have sinned, save for Mary who was preserved from original sin and never committed a personal sin. Regardless of how perfect any human being is or may seem they are not worthy of adoration or worship, only God should be worshiped.

However, we can venerate and follow the example of the Canonized saints, because the church has declared that without a doubt they are in heaven. They are not dead, but more alive than we are because they possess eternal life and are a triumphant member of the Body of Christ. Let me give you a personal example to explain what I mean by venerating the saints.

My Grandmother was my Confirmation sponsor, and I relied on her to mentor me in the faith. About a year ago, I called her, and I asked her to pray for me and talk through a difficult situation in my life as a 30-something year old guy. I needed her prayers, advice, and encouragement.

During the conversation I told her I called because she was my Confirmation sponsor. I venerated that role she played in the development of my faith, and because of that it elevated that conversation from a mere show of support into a powerful Holy Spirit-infused conversation. Simply, I recognized at a young age that my Grandmother had a special connection to the Holy Spirit, and I knew that I would be able to rely on her to share that gift with me!

Likewise, we venerate Saints because of their holiness of life and their communion with God in heaven. This closeness to God allows us to ask for their prayers.

_____

Editor's Note: The biblical commandment forbidding images of God has been superseded by the incarnation of Jesus, Who, as the Second Person of the Trinity, is God incarnate in visible matter. Therefore, we are not depicting an invisible God (an idol), but God as He appeared in the flesh. This was decreed by the Second Ecumenical Council of Nicaea in 787 and upheld by Pope Gregory II. Our belief is that when we venerate an icon, our veneration proceeds to the person depicted by the icon.

Why Does God Permit Bad Things in Our World?

5.   *Why does God let bad things happen in our world?*

A.   It really comes down to love. I know that sounds silly, but you cannot force someone to love you, and neither can God. God gave us free will hoping that we would freely choose to love Him. The good news is we can choose to love Him, and the bad news is we can also choose not to love Him. If God created us without free will love simply wouldn't exist.

So how about the things we cannot control then, like destructive forces of nature or the global coronavirus pandemic that we suffered? Well, do you remember in the Garden of Eden that God said we had dominion over nature? What did that mean? It meant that God gave us the role of steward of creation. We were entrusted with taking care of it and when we sinned against God, we also abandoned our duty to our stewardship of the created world. Therefore, all of the created world "followed our lead" in a certain sense and rebelled against God as well. As a result, every living thing experiences death and the forces of nature can inflict devastation upon the earth, all through our sin.

If that still seems a little lacking, the Church recognizes that no answer will fully satisfy us now, but we will eventually know the reasons for all of it when we get to Heaven. "We firmly believe that God is the master of the world and its history. But the ways of His providence are often unknown to us. Only at the end, when our partial knowledge ceases, when we see God "face to face," will we fully know the ways by which – even through the dramas of evil and sin – God has guided His creation to that definitive sabbath rest for which He created heaven and earth." (CCC 314)

Creation vs. Science

6.   *How does the Church's teachings on Creation not contradict, but build upon while preserving the integrity of, scientific theories such as the Big Bang or Evolution?*

A.   I'm glad you used the Big Bang Theory in your question as an example. Why am I so happy? Because the most important title that Georges Lemaître, the Belgian scientist who first developed the theory in 1931, held is readily omitted from the discussion. What is that title you ask?

Father. Yes, Fr. Georges Lemaître was a Catholic priest and scientist. Does that information change your perception of the Big Bang Theory? Does it inspire you to learn more about the theory? It should.

With that said, Theology and science are distinct disciplines. Theology is the study of God using reason, Divine Revelation and the Magisterium of the Catholic Church. Science seeks to understand natural phenomena by means of the scientific method. Science does not utilize the data of Revelation in formulating its conclusions.

Recognizing the need for faith-based scientific

research that is both grounded in the moral and ethical teachings of Christ and the Catholic Church and groundbreaking in its discovery of new scientific theories, Pope Pius XI established the Pontifical Academy of Sciences in 1936 at the Vatican and continues to do great work today.

Simply, scientists who respect Divine Revelation in their work advance scientific research in a positive way and help people live their lives abundantly. This idea is summed up and supported by the teaching of the Church in the Catechism.

"Faith and science: Though faith is above reason, there can never be any real discrepancy between faith and reason. Since the same God who reveals mysteries and infuses faith has bestowed the light of reason on the human mind, God cannot deny Himself, nor can truth ever contradict truth.

Consequently, methodical research in all branches of knowledge, provided it is carried out in a truly scientific manner and does not override moral laws, can never conflict with the faith, because the things of the world and the things of faith derive from the same God. The humble and persevering investigator of the secrets of nature is being led, as it were, by the hand of God in spite of himself, for it is God, the conserver of all things, who made them what they are." (CCC 159)

Guided Interpretation of Biblical Languages

7.   *When theologians explain Scripture, they sometimes interpret the meaning of passages by the original translation and etymology of particular words, which vary between different languages, including Greek, Hebrew, and Latin. How do they know which language to translate the words back into, and how does that result in different versions of the Bible?*

A.   If you look in the front of Catholic bibles you are going to see a statement that says, "translated from original languages with critical use of all the ancient sources," or something similar. When the Catholic Church translates the bible, the Confraternity of Christian Doctrine takes great care to employ numerous biblical scholars, historians and language experts and this helps to ensure that the translation is accurate and faithful to the Magisterium. If you are interested in who is on this team, their names, credentials and roles are most likely printed in the front of your Catholic Bible.

Keep in mind however that their work will be lacking in some way, no matter how credentialed they are because they are limited by a finite language to express the infinite wisdom and love of God.

Different translations and footnotes can help us dive deeper into the mystery of God and help us express the inexpressible a little more fully, though never completely.

Denominational vs. Catholic Bibles

8.   *Are there versions of the Bible that are exclusive for different denominations?*

A.   There are literally thousands of translations of the Bible, especially Protestant Bibles. There are fewer approved translations of the Catholic Bible, because of the process we explained in the previous question. Some include the New American Bible, the Revised Standard Version, and the Douay-Rheims. The Catholic Bible has 73 books, whereas most Protestant Bibles such as the King James Version have seven fewer books. There are also Bibles associated with denominations such as several versions for those who consider themselves "Evangelicals." An approved Catholic translation of the Bible is recommended as it contains the entire canon, is consistent with Church teaching, and has been approved by the bishops.

There is a long history as to why Catholics have more books in the Bible. The basics are it has to do with the fact that shortly after the time of Jesus around 90 A.D., a group of Jewish scholars gathered together and debated which books of the Old Testament were the inspired Word of God.

This debate didn't take place in the early Christian church because it was not a matter of discussion among early Christians, but rather Jews. The decision of most Jews (but not all), after the time of Christ to make changes to their canon, had and still has no impact on the canon of Catholic Christian Scripture. Early Christians believed the Deuterocanonical books to be the inspired word of God and the teachings formed the foundation of our beliefs as Catholics.

Martin Luther, during the period of the protestant reformation eliminated these books from his Bible because the teaching contained within them contradicted teachings of the Catholic Church he disagreed with and claimed that the Jews didn't see them as the inspired word of God.

Catholics, LGBTQ, and Same Sex Marriage

9.   *One of the most controversial teachings of the Church is on gay marriage. What is the distinction between the condemnation of the action versus the person? What makes the Catholic teaching on homosexuality one of love and not of bigotry?*

God gives us the gift of sexual intercourse to be co-creators of life with Him. It is beautiful, wonderful and incredible when shared on the proper canvas of marriage. However, when we make a conscious decision to ignore His guidance and instruction, we taint this good gift.

Sexual acts outside a valid marriage and sexual acts within marriage that are not open to life, have a negative impact on the beautiful image God is trying to create through us with His gift of sexuality. The Church is not singling anyone out – heterosexual and homosexual alike, if you are having sex outside marriage, you are using the gift of your sexuality improperly. This includes, pre-marital sex, extra-marital affairs, using contraception (both chemical and physical barriers) masturbation and pornography. Take note that even within a valid marriage sexual sin can be present, through masturbation, contraception, extra-marital affairs, and pornography.

In the case of homosexuality, because the sexual acts are contrary to nature and have no possibility of creating a new life, then the homosexual couple cannot properly consummate a marriage and cannot be married in God's eyes (even if it has become accepted by our society). Therefore, all homosexual acts are inherently sinful.

Notice, that I said homosexual acts, not those who experience homosexual tendencies or inclinations. Men and women who may struggle with same-sex attraction are deserving of God's love and ours, to be treated with dignity, and welcomed into our faith communities.

However, forces within our society like Hollywood, the media, and the redefinition of marriage by the state has made it more challenging to minister to those inclined to this sin because they have declared this sin a good. Celebrating human weakness as a good has led many to be confused.

Most people (but not all) who experience same-sex attraction claim it is not a choice and they were born with them. While we must respect this personal perspective, science has yet to find a gay gene or know how it comes about in one's psyche and as the catechism correctly states its genesis is "largely unexplained (CCC 2357)."

The bottom line is it does not matter whether we were born with our weaknesses or acquired them, we must call them weaknesses because that is what they are, otherwise pride will prevent us from receiving true compassion from God.

St. Paul says, "power is made perfect in weakness therefore I will boast of my weaknesses (cf. 2 Cor 12:9)." And we need to listen to what that means from a scriptural perspective in this instance. True authentic self-compassion is when we can admit to God and others that we struggle with our weakness whatever it might be, and while we may never fully "conquer the weakness" in our lifetime we need to admit that it is a weakness, not a strength.

Satan tries to confuse us into celebrating the weakness that we struggle with as a good thing rather than allowing God to powerfully use our weakness for good. There is a big difference between those two.

The current cultural climate does make it more difficult for people struggling with this to avoid the near occasion of sin, but the truth is it isn't impossible for people who regularly struggle with the sin of committing homosexual acts to live a chaste life; especially when that person relies on the infinite mercy and grace of God.

God never created someone that He didn't completely and unconditionally love, but He doesn't embrace their sin or the things that lead them toward it. Rather He forgives sins and instructs us to pray, "lead us not into temptation (cf Matt 6:13)." Christ is the perfect model when it comes to counseling someone struggling with this (and all sin) and engaging in its surrounding culture.

A final note on bigotry, Pope St. John Paull II once said at World Youth Day in Toronto in 2002, "We are not the sum of our weaknesses and failures, we are the sum of the Father's love for us and our real capacity to become the image of His Son Jesus." With that in mind, we aren't called to judge others on their weaknesses or sins.

We don't need to be standing there with a clipboard tallying how many times our friends or acquaintances have fallen into a particular sin, and I'm sure you don't want someone doing the same thing when you fall into a sin you struggle with regularly. Rather, we are called to love all people in a radical way, to show them how much they are loved by the Father and help them discover their capacity to become the image of Jesus in the world. Truth cannot be bigoted.

Are some sins greater than others? *Yes.*

Are we called to stand for the truth of our faith no matter how much it confounds the world? *Yes.*

Are we called to radically love one another? *Yes.*

What does that look like?
Being the image of Jesus.

If someone you know is struggling with a habitual sexual sin and confides in you, take the opportunity to remind them they are loved by God. Help them peel off the label that reduces their complex identity to their sin. God knows their weaknesses, faults, and sinful inclinations and does not label them by it but chooses to call them by name to become more like His Son, Jesus.

Even if they disagree with you about it being "bad" for them to misuse their gift of sexuality, you will be able to show them that you do not hate them or dislike them, that you only want what is best for them and that they can trust you as a friend. This is what it means to be the image of Jesus in the world.

If they choose to distance themselves or walk away from you entirely that is unfortunate – and it is on them – you have loved to the best of your ability, and you are not a bigot for loving them in truth.

10

Sex and Infertility

10. *Stemming off the previous question, my general understanding of why the Church does not support gay marriage is because marriage is intended to be unitive and procreative. To summarize, the purpose of marriage is to have children and a gay couple cannot do this naturally. My question is, though, does this same concept apply to a married heterosexual couple that is infertile? If it is said by doctors that this couple cannot naturally create children, does this make their marriage and/or sexual life sinful?*

A.   You are right in saying that the sexual act both must be unitive and procreative to be ordered properly, but the purpose of Marriage is for a husband and wife to be a witness or mirror of God's love in the world, part of that plan is being "open" to having children (meaning not using contraception within marriage or aborting a pre-born child). Children or lack thereof don't impact the validity or purpose of the Sacrament of Matrimony.

Many couples get validly married after the childbearing years of a woman are considered long past, or they struggle with infertility as you mentioned, but neither are sinful.

Remember two biblical stories here, first that of Abraham and Sarah. Sarah believed that she was too old to have children and bore a son Isaac. Isaac went on to be the first of descendants as numerous as the stars for his parents Abraham and Sarah.

The second, that of St. Elizabeth, who was called barren or infertile. Her son was St. John the Baptist, the person who would prepare the way for Jesus. When we are open to God's plan, nothing is impossible for Him.

Finally, God fully expects us to love our spouses in a sexual way, God's first words to man in the Bible are "be fruitful and multiply, fill the earth and subdue it." Sex, when it is properly ordered within marriage (open to life by not using contraception) is a regular, natural, and beautiful part of the relationship.

While a heterosexual couple may never actually procreate, the key is that there's a chance because of God's design for their bodies and because the couple has an openness to the possibility of their sexual act resulting in the creation of new life.

Catholic Stand
on the Death Penalty

11.   *What does the Church believe about the death penalty? Is it purely wrong to end another human's life or is it circumstantial?*

A.   For a long time, the Catholic Church held the belief and reserved the death penalty if it was the only possible way "of effectively defending human lives against the unjust aggressor," and the "cases in which the execution of the offender is an absolute necessity are rare, if practically non-existent." (cf. CCC 2267 – ed. 1994)

However, in 2018 at the direction of Pope Francis, the Church updated the Catechism to reflect a new teaching on the death penalty, making it inadmissible in every circumstance. This update has deepened the Church's teaching on the practice and says:

"Recourse to the death penalty on the part of legitimate authority, following a fair trial, was long considered an appropriate response to the gravity of certain crimes and an acceptable, albeit extreme, means of safeguarding the common good.

Today, however, there is an increasing awareness that the dignity of the person is not lost even after the commission of profoundly serious crimes. In addition, a new understanding has emerged of the significance of penal sanctions imposed by the state. Lastly, more effective systems of detention have been developed, which ensure the due protection of citizens but, at the same time, do not definitively deprive the guilty of the possibility of redemption.

Consequently, the Church teaches, in the light of the Gospel, that 'the death penalty is inadmissible because it is an attack on the inviolability and dignity of the person,' and she works with determination for its abolition worldwide." (CCC 2267 – ed. 2018)

This deepening of Church teaching is just one example of how the Church is listening to the active voice of the Holy Spirit to help the faithful grow in Holiness.

Catholic Response to Non-Pro-Life Persons

12.   *How can I respond to someone that is against my Pro-Life stance per the Catholic teaching on abortion?*

A.   I'm glad that your pro-life stance of being is non-negotiable. That being said, I think how you respond to someone who doesn't share your views on the sanctity of life largely depends on your situation and personality.

Are you encountering pro-abortion supporters at the March for Life and are they antagonizing you? Are you at a coffee shop debating this with a close friend? I think it is important for you to evaluate your environment, the temperament of those you are talking to and pray about the right thing to do in that circumstance. Personally, I pray about what is going to make the biggest impact. If the person is an angry protester and screaming "keep your rosaries off my ovaries" at you, the best thing to probably do in that situation is not engage the person but offer a quiet prayer for them – my prayer for their conversion of heart I believe is greater than confronting or arguing with them.

However, if I'm talking with someone who has a greater chance of listening to what I have to say, I'll engage in a civil conversation with them. I think that in this case it is important to engage in active listening and prayer during the conversation. There is a reason why the Holy Spirit has provided an opportunity for you to talk with that person and by listening to them, their viewpoint and personal experience while asking the Holy Spirit for guidance God will work through you to convey a message of love and hope for them to think about. Don't worry about changing their heart or mind only God can do that.

Explaining Why
Deacons Can Marry

13.   *Why are deacons able to get married but not priests?*

A.   Celibacy is a discipline in the Roman Catholic Church. This means that it does not impede the person from the reception of Holy Orders. Disciplines are laws and directions set down by Church authority for the guidance of the faithful[1]. In other words, because it is a discipline, and not a teaching of Jesus or dogma of the faith that only unmarried celibate men can be admitted to the Sacrament of Holy Orders, then there and can be exceptions to this practice.

During the Second Vatican Council this practice was examined in depth because some in the church wanted to relax the discipline and make it optional. "Recognizing the grave shortage of priests in many countries compared to the number of professed Catholics, the Council authorized the permanent deaconate and allowed these permanent deacons to be ordained as married men. But it remained inflexible on priestly celibacy (Clerical Celibacy - The Catholic Catechism by John A Hardon, SJ)."

A permanent deacon is ordained to serve the church by reaching the marginalized, baptize, witness the sacrament of Holy Matrimony, proclaim the Gospel, assist and preach at the Mass. Finally, permanent deacons must be married prior to being ordained and if their wife dies, they cannot remarry.

---

[1]https://www.catholicculture.org/culture/library/dictionary/index.cfm?id=33114

Are Outdoor Masses or Weddings Permitted?

14. *Are outdoor Masses allowed? How about weddings?*

A.   Canon Law states: "The Eucharistic celebration is to be carried out in a sacred place unless in a particular necessity requires otherwise; in such a case the celebration must be done in a decent place (Cannon 932: #1)." In the case of necessity, outdoor Masses along with Masses in airports, hotel conference centers and even the hood of a military vehicle (there is a famous photo of Fr. Gerald Clune celebrating Mass on the hood of a car during the Korean war) are permitted in most circumstances.

However, when it comes to weddings, the building is important. The Church is a central symbol because the family is the domestic Church. The husband and wife mirror the Church's relationship with Christ and the Trinity. Because the building is such a central symbol of this witness of the husband and wife weddings must take place inside of a church building.

One other thing to remember is that every Sacrament has a public nature to it, therefore the public should be aware that you are celebrating the Sacrament so people can attend if they would like to do so.

Sharing the Same Cup at Mass

15.   *Why does everyone share the same cup for the precious blood at Mass?*

A.   Simply, Jesus commanded the apostles to drink of the one cup of His Blood. These are part of the words of institution and can't be changed. We are re-presenting the last supper at every Mass and therefore drink of the blood from the communal cup.

Also, because we worship and adore the Blessed Sacrament as the very flesh and blood of God, He deserves to be honored by giving Him our best, thus it isn't appropriate to offer the Blessed Sacrament in individual dixie cups.

16

What About Purgatory?

16.   *Is Purgatory talked about in the Bible?*

A.   If you are looking for an explicit mention of
Purgatory, you will not find it the Bible. However, there
are several references to a place of purgation throughout
both the Old and New Testaments. Here are a couple of
examples worthy of reflection:

"But who can endure the day of His coming? Who
can stand firm when He appears? For He will be like a
refiner's fire, like a fuller's lye. He will sit refining and
purifying silver and He will purify the Levites, refining
them like gold or silver that they may bring offerings to the
Lord in righteousness." (Malachi 3:2-3)

"Settle with your opponent quickly on your way
to court with him. Otherwise, your opponent will hand you
over to the judge and the judge will hand you over to the
guard and you will be thrown into prison. Amen, I say to
you, you will not be released until you have paid the last
penny." (Matthew 5:25-26)

Some other scripture passages that reference purgatory are:

2 Macc. 13:23-26

Tob. 4:18

Ecc. 7:37

Ps. 65:12

Matt 12:32

Beyond the many scriptural references, the doctrine of Purgatory has been reinforced by some of the greatest saints in our history and referenced several Church-approved Marian apparitions. When we understand what Purgatory is, it also makes a lot of sense.

Imagine this scenario, you throw a rock through your neighbor's window. You've sinned and broken the window. If you don't go over and apologize that relationship is severed forever – in spiritual terms you are going to Hell.

However, you do go over and apologize, and your neighbor forgives you. The relationship has been restored. You are no longer going to Hell; however, your neighbor still has a broken window that needs to be repaired. In order to enter Heaven, you can't have any outstanding debts to pay.

This is where Purgatory comes into play. It's a place to pay off your spiritual debts. It's an uncomfortable and painful process but necessary and is why the priest gives you a penance after you've confessed your sins in the sacrament of Reconciliation. We can do our best to avoid Purgatory by offering prayers and doing penance throughout our lives, but the reality is we will most likely need to repair a few windows.

Date Set for
Mary's Assumption

17. *Why do we celebrate the Assumption of Mary
on August 15th?*

A.   The assumption of the Blessed Virgin Mary has
been celebrated for millennium by the faithful but was
promulgated as a dogma relatively recently by Pope Pius
XII on November 1, 1950. We celebrate this teaching of
the Church for a few reasons. First, to honor the Blessed
Virgin Mary's sinless life. In her perfection she was
rewarded with an immediate entry into heaven body and
soul and didn't have to wait for her body to be reunited
with her soul at the time of the second coming.

Also, this solemnity helps us anticipate what will
happen to all the redeemed at the end of time;
reminding us that our bodies are a temple of the Holy
Spirit and that we too will be taken up body and soul
into heaven. Therefore, we are to treat both our body
and others' bodies with respect and dignity. By taking
care of the body, we are given by God, we like Mary, at
the end of time we will be reunited with our glorified
body.

Catholics and the Separation of Church and State

18. *What is the Church's belief on the separation of Church and state?*

A.   The Catholic Church is a worldwide institution, and it predates the formation of the United States as a country and therefore doesn't comment directly on the Constitution (or the governing principles or laws of other countries for that matter). However, it does clearly express the necessity to have a government and gives principles for how that government should operate.

The Catechism of the Catholic Church states:

"Certain societies, such as the family and the state, correspond more directly to the nature of man; they are necessary to him. To promote the participation of the greatest number in the life of a society, the creation of voluntary associations and institutions must be encouraged 'on both national and international levels, which relate to economic and social goals, to cultural and recreational activities, to sport, to various professions, and to political affairs.' This 'socialization' also expresses the natural tendency for human beings to associate with one another for the sake of attaining objectives that exceed individual capacities. It develops the qualities of the person, especially the sense of initiative and responsibility, and helps guarantee his rights. Socialization also presents dangers. Excessive intervention by the state can threaten personal freedom and initiative. The teaching of the Church has elaborated the principle of subsidiarity, according to which a community of a higher order should not interfere in the internal life of a community of a lower order, depriving the latter of its functions, but rather should support it in case of need and help to co-ordinate its activity with the activities of the rest of society, always with a view to the common good. God has not willed to reserve to Himself all exercise of power. He entrusts to every creature the functions it is capable of performing, according to the capacities of its own nature. This mode of governance ought to be followed in social life. The way God acts in governing the world, which bears witness to such great regard for human freedom, should inspire the wisdom of those who govern human communities. They should behave as ministers of divine providence." (cf. CCC 1882-1884)

The above quote stresses above all that the freedom of the human person must not be excessively controlled by the state. Our freedom is not a right because the state has decided to give it to us, rather God has created us to be free and governments are responsible to ensure its citizens are afforded that freedom.

Pro-Life Focus
Should Be All-Inclusive

19. *Why are most pro-life movements and marches only focusing on abolishing abortion? When I attended the March for Life, I wondered why every sign I saw was about protecting unborn lives rather than focusing on all life stages and pro-life focuses. I did not see any signs about the death penalty, physician-assisted suicide, euthanasia, or other pro-life issues.*

You bring up a great point, we as Catholics do have a responsibility to draw awareness to and work to end injustices of all kinds, especially those that deal with terminating life before a natural death. Regarding the death penalty specifically, the Catholic Mobilizing Network is a great organization that works to end the death penalty, but certainly more can be done to promote the consistent ethic of life throughout the Church.

Perhaps this is an area where you can lead the Church, if you are passionate about one of these issues, I encourage you to start your own non-profit organization, talk to your local diocese about the resources they have and get involved. Simply, we need you to put your faith into action!

Morality of
Unnecessary Purchases

20.   *Is it immoral to buy things you don't need?*

A.   It is not "immoral" to buy things you don't need, but as Catholics we should always strive to be good stewards so we should do our best to have money to also give to our Church, charities, and/or help the poor. It is always a better choice to be frugal and to attempt to pay less for items if possible to be better stewards of the money God has granted us. We are blessed with all that God provides in our lives. Perhaps the bigger picture is how can we use our gifts to enrich the lives of others. (Greed is a deadly sin). Prayer and discernment *is* the best practice to make good choices when it comes to stewardship.

Living Together
Before Marriage

21.   *Why can't I live together before getting*
       married? It seems like it's impractical these
       days to wait. Wouldn't we be a lot better off
       testing our compatibility and sound financial
       foundation to enter life together? Why wait?

A.   As we mentioned in a few of the previous
questions regarding sexuality, God doesn't want you
to have sex before marriage. Putting yourself in a
situation where you are living with someone you are
physically and emotionally attracted is to surround
yourself in a constant state of temptation. It can also be a
cause of scandal because friends and acquaintances
might just presume that you are having sex. But let us say
for the sake of the argument you were able to completely
avoid premarital sex, should you live together prior
to marriage?

       Marriage is a sacrament; it gives supernatural
grace to the recipients. Meaning that when your better half
asks you to do the dishes every night for seven consecutive
weeks, constantly pick your socks up off the floor or run
to the store at 1:30 a.m., you will have the grace to realize

they aren't being selfish or asking too much of you because you made a lifelong vow to love and honor them all the days of their lives.

Without this lifelong commitment in place, it is a lot easier to be selfish, not be fully transparent in your relationship and intentionally hide your character defects because you are trying to impress your partner. In other words, even though your proximity to the person is closer physically it is easier to hide the character flaws and not be your true self.

There is also research to back this up. The Journal of Marriage and Family published a study in September of 2018 by Michael J. Rosenfeld and Katharena Roesler with the conclusion that couples that cohabitate prior to marriage have a higher divorce rate. A simple internet search of their work entitled "Cohabitation Experience and Cohabitation's Association with Marital Dissolution[1]" will give you access to their study and extensive research.

Marriage is incredibly simple, yet profoundly challenging. Simply, the grace of the Sacrament is needed to draw two flawed people together so that in turn God can transform their union into a beautiful life-giving relationship and foundation for Him to raise new disciples and build His kingdom. If we make the decision to skip the grace of the Sacrament before we live together and then only show the good parts of ourselves to our partners, it is a recipe for disaster and can lead to divorce.

---

[1] https://onlinelibrary.wiley.com/doi/abs/10.1111/jomf.1253
0?af=R

22

Underage Drinking

22.   *Is it sinful to drink underage?*

A.   Underage drinking is against the civil law of most states and US territories, and it is up to each individual state to define and enforce this law. A simple internet search will reveal the statutes of the state in which you reside (while 21 is generally the legal age to consume alcohol there are some nuances to the laws that differ by state or territory).

Unlike civil laws that contradict the natural law (i.e., the right to abortion) which must be opposed, Human laws that do not contradict natural law are binding on the conscience. Scripture confirms that civil authorities derive their legitimate authority from God; "Let every person be subordinate to the higher authorities, for there is no authority except from God. Therefore, whoever resists authority opposes what God has appointed, and those who oppose it will bring judgement upon themselves. For rulers are not a cause of fear to good conduct, but to evil (Romans 13:1-3)."

In other words, Governments have a moral responsibility to safeguard the common good of its citizens through the rule of law and setting a minimum age to consume alcohol can be seen as protecting the common good of society. Simply because they are just laws, it is sinful to disobey underage drinking laws.

Remember, it is easy to obey laws and rules that you agree with, but a true test of character is to obey those we do not like. While it might be quite unpopular, obedience does not ask your opinion or ours. Therefore, we will refrain from sharing what we personally think about the law.

Also keep in mind, that when it comes to drinking alcohol, Scripture says in numerous places we should not get drunk. We are morally obligated by God to not drink to the point that we are intoxicated, and our inhibitions are lowered and unable to make sound moral judgments. If you do so, you have committed sin no matter your age.

Catholic Political Decisions   23

23.   *Is there a certain political party Catholics
should identify with? When considering the
pro-life movement when supporting a specific
political party, how can one choose between
Republicans, when they typically do not
support abortion but support the death
penalty, and Democrats, when they typically
do support abortion but do not support
the death penalty?*

A.   The Church does not have or endorse a political
party. With that said, the United States Conferences of
Catholic Bishops on November 11, 2019 stated in their
introductory letter of their most recent update to the voting
guide, *Forming Consciences for Faithful Citizenship*: "The
threat of abortion remains our preeminent priority because
it directly attacks life itself, because it takes place within
the sanctuary of the family, and because of the number of
lives destroyed. At the same time, we cannot dismiss or

ignore other serious threats to human life and dignity such as racism, the environmental crisis, poverty and the death penalty."

Simply, there are certain moral issues that are non-negotiable, protecting innocent unborn life is at the top of the list, but all issues related to basic human rights should be considered when voting.

Perhaps the best answer is not to choose between political parties but to choose between which candidates respect and uphold laws which protect the most vulnerable members of society.

Unfortunately, in today's political quagmire, there are challenges for those who wish to vote pro-life when some candidates may be pro-life when it comes to abortion and but not so much with the death penalty or other areas such as euthanasia, or physician-assisted suicide.

Being Catholic and upholding moral law encompasses varied areas of consideration and we are obligated to rigorously examine the candidates, the issues at stake in the election and ourselves before voting. Pope St. John Paul II gives some great perspective about how the actions, or lack thereof of, individuals toward defending the most vulnerable in society contributes to collective social sin:

"Also social is every sin against the rights of the human person, beginning with the right to life and including the life of the unborn or against a person's integrity...

The term social can be applied to sins of commission or omission – on the part of political, economic or trade union leaders, who though in a position to do so, do not work diligently and wisely for the improvement and transformation of society according to the requirements and potential of the given historic moment... Whenever the Church speaks of situations of sin or when the condemns as social sins certain situations or the collective behavior of certain social groups, big or small, or even of whole nations and blocs of nations, she knows and she proclaims that such cases of social sin are the result of the accumulation and concentration of many personal sins. It is a case of the very personal sins of those who cause or support evil or who exploit it; of those who are in a position to avoid, eliminate or at least limit certain social evils but who fail to do so out of laziness, fear or the conspiracy of silence, through secret complicity or indifference; of those who take refuge in the supposed impossibility of changing the world and also of those who sidestep the effort and sacrifice required, producing specious reasons of a higher order. The real responsibility, then, lies with individuals."[2]

Voting is one way that we put our faith into action and by forming our conscience well before doing so ensures that we contribute to the building up of society, not its destruction.

---

[2] Pope John Paul II, Reconciliation and Penance (1984), no. 16.

Representations of Jesus & Interpreting the Transfiguration Account

24. *Why do common depictions and artworks of Jesus portray Him as white and with blue eyes? Through research it can be deducted that a Jewish Galilean from 2,000 years ago had darker skin and darker eyes. Revelation 1:14-15 says, "His head and His hairs were white like wool, as white as snow; and His eyes were as a flame of fire; And His feet like unto fine brass, as if they burned in a furnace," describing Jesus as having darker features.*

A.   Simply, Jesus was a Jewish man. Therefore, His skin color and characteristics would have resembled that of a Jewish man in that time period. As far as the many types of depictions of Jesus including that of a white male, throughout the world there are several different depictions of our Blessed Mother that of a Hispanic woman, African, Asian and many others.

There are also several different depictions of Jesus as a man of many different cultures. He is depicted this way in the artwork of the various cultures throughout history. Different cultures portray Him in various ways.

To reflect on the scriptural quote in the question and an explanation:

"His head and His hairs were white like wool, as white as snow; and His eyes were as a flame of fire; And His feet like unto fine brass, as if they burned in a furnace."

This description is similar to how Jesus appeared during the Transfiguration from the New Testament.

The appearance of Jesus in this scriptural passage is that of His heavenly body, much different than His earthly appearance.

Jesus is fully human and fully divine. In reading Scripture, we must remember some depictions such as the one above, reveal a more "divine" image, but we know in appearance He was a Jewish male in His humanity.

For further reading, the Transfiguration can be found in Scripture in Matthew 17:1-8, Mark 9:2-8, Luke 9:28-36) describe it, and the Second Epistle of Peter also refers to it. (2 Peter 1:16-18)

The Church & Marijuana Use

25.   *What is the Catholic Church's stance on marijuana? It is legal in certain states and countries. It is used for medical reasons, in social contexts, and to achieve relaxation. While it used to be seen as a "bad drug," it is now widely accepted as a good thing for individuals and for society. What should my approach be to this as a Catholic?*

A.   As we've stated in some of the other questions, just because it is legal, or society declares it a good, it doesn't make it right or moral. Scripture reminds us to "be sober and vigilant. Your opponent the devil is prowling around like a roaring lion looking for someone to devour. Resist him steadfast in faith, knowing your fellow believers undergo the same sufferings (1 Peter 5:8-9)." This applies to our relationship with marijuana as a Catholic. From what we know about marijuana, it impairs us from making sound and effective moral decisions and it should be avoided recreationally. We have an obligation to God to live soberly and the use of marijuana can provide a foothold for Satan to enter our souls and wreak more havoc upon us. In the sense of medical usage, could a case be

allowed under the strict care of medical professionals?
It might be considered reasonable, however with the
advancements with pain management drugs that we
have available today it is not a necessity.

Also, keep in mind that physical suffering has an
important purpose in our lives and can help us grow closer
in our relationship with God. God's plan of salvation didn't
include transporting our minds to an altered state or
magically doing away with all our pain, rather He showed
us He was willing to become one of us, experience the
human condition and redeem us by suffering an
excruciating death for us.

Jesus says, "whoever does not take up his cross and
follow after Me is not worthy of Me," (Matthew 10:38) and
so finding a constant escape of our pain through drugs (or
excessive use of alcohol) whether it be emotional or
physical is not appropriate for disciples of Christ and
certainly sinful.

The Catechism confirms:

"The use of drugs inflicts very grave damage on
human health and life. Their use, except on strictly
therapeutic grounds, is a grave offense. Clandestine
production of and trafficking in drugs are scandalous
practices. They constitute direct cooperation in evil,
since they encourage people to practices gravely contrary
to the moral law." (CCC 2291)

Meeting Like-Minded Catholics

26.

26.   *How do I meet like-minded people of faith who want to practice Catholicism?*

A.   As a college student, you are likely surrounded by peers with a wide variety of beliefs, values, and lifestyles. College is a unique time to allow the Holy Spirit to work in and through relationships with people who might have completely different ideals than you. I recommend embracing these types of relationships as much as possible and being extra attentive to God's presence in them!

That being said, it is absolutely beneficial to meet people with whom you already share common ground and find awesome synergy while building upon that foundation together. If your college or university has a Campus Ministry department, Catholic Student Association, or Newman Club, you already have a structure through which you can find those like-minded peers. If your school doesn't have any of those, consider taking a leap and asking your school if you can start one – chances are there are other like-minded students who are hoping to meet you too!

There are often opportunities for young adults through your local diocese, as well, and if there aren't, consider taking a lead on making them happen. There are, of course, always ways to get connected with like-minded people of faith online. There are so many social media pages and websites that allow for connections to happen – don't shy away from them! Whatever the setting, it will likely take initiative and patience on your part to forge these relationships.

If you're a Catholic looking to meet other Catholics, strike up a conversation after Mass with someone new, mingle at a "Theology on Tap" event, or reach out to other Catholics in your local area through social media and suggest an appropriate meet-up. There are several social media pages, specifically designed by young Catholics, which are dedicated to helping other young Catholics find each other. "Nashville Catholic Young Adults," "San Diego Catholic Adult Community – Young Adults," "Catholic Young Adults of Bucks County," and "Disney College Program – Catholics" are a few random examples.

Respond to Time Issues

27.   *If somebody says that they cannot attend Mass on Sunday because they have too much homework, how could I respond?*

A.   With gentleness! Your response should be appropriate and proportional to the relationship. If a person is saying this directly to you, I assume you already have a relationship with him or her.

Hopefully, your response would look different for an acquaintance than it would for a close friend. Going to Mass every Sunday and thereby "fulfilling your Sunday obligation" can be challenging for college students who are trying to hold so much in balance. They also might not see the "obligation" as an *opportunity* to be inspired by God, to praise God with a supportive and unified community, and to get into a good space in preparation for the week ahead.

When you respond to people who say they cannot attend Mass due to homework or any other cause for "busyness," you walk a fine line between being dismissive and being judgmental. On one hand, you don't want to encourage a person's decision to miss out on this valuable time with God and a community of worshippers. On the other hand, you also don't want to risk coming off as judgmental or "holier than thou" – this might discourage a person from participating in future Masses because they are bitter towards the community or perceive themselves as being "not holy enough," and thus have a relationship with him or her.

Hopefully your response to an acquaintance could be something along the lines of "I'm sorry you're so busy with homework. It can be so difficult to make it all happen. For me, I always find it easier to hit the ground running with homework after I have an hour at Mass where I can just shut the homework part of my brain down. I forget homework exists for an hour and then I'm fueled to get it done after."

Humility in Evangelization

28. *How do you practice humility in evangelization? It is hard to distinguish whether I am sharing my faith or simply showing off my knowledge of the Faith. How do you prevent any success in evangelization from feeding your ego?*

A.   Humility is such a beautiful virtue that can be very difficult to put into practice. *How* you share your Faith is *absolutely* key.

Meeting people where they are, without shying away from (or compromising) the Truth is a skill that everybody should continue to hone throughout their lives.

Humility, living in self-truthfulness, involves self-reflection. Don't feel guilty for being proud of yourself for the positive role you have had in somebody's life. Many times, those "evangelization moments" happen not necessarily when you approach someone, but when that someone approaches you – he or she sees something attractive – something Christ-like! Reflecting God and cooperating with Him is certainly something to feel good about.

When you feel that sense of accomplishment, you might keep your ego in check by silently thanking God for the grace He has given you to be able to spread the Good News. Expressing gratitude for the gifts of the Holy Spirit, whether to God, or in response to a compliment from someone else, is a great way to lift the credit off yourself and direct it back to the ultimate source of wisdom and counsel.

First Encounters

29. *How do I spread positivity about the Catholic faith when I first meet someone? It seems that whenever I meet someone (at work, in school, at events, etc.) who is not religious and they find out I am Catholic, I usually get a seemingly negative response as if they feel sorry for me. I usually hear the unenthusiastic "oh wow" and see their eyes veer off to the side. I do my best to stay happy and cheerful about how I love that is a part of my identity, but I don't know how else to address this.*

A.   It is so unfortunate that being Catholic invokes pity from some. However, this initial response from someone can provide an excellent opportunity for building understanding and planting seeds to shift someone's perspective. It can often feel like there's so much to defend when you get this reaction – don't feel overwhelmed.

   Focus on maximizing this opportunity to plant a simple seed of joy. When faced with this reaction, it's easy to respond back with one of two extremes: becoming overly defensive, thus creating an impression that the Church has "brainwashed" you into defending it or carrying on the conversation without acknowledging the other person's reaction (AKA rolling over and playing dead), thus creating an impression that their reaction was warranted.

Sometimes something as simple as "I love my faith...," followed by "it's gotten me through a lot in my life," "it gives me a sense of hope," "I've found peace through it," etc., makes a lasting impact on someone you first meet. No one can disagree with your personal experience. If you make it about your experience, it will at the very least allow the person to think twice about how their impression of the Church isn't everyone else's.

At best, it will propel further discussion, and hopefully give you some insight as to what the other person's experiences or impressions have been. If this discussion progresses, you might have some opportunities to address misconceptions, or highlight specific elements about being Catholic that you enjoy.

The goal here isn't to convert the other person, it is simply to build understanding. Whether your interaction grows into a discussion or stops after a few words are exchanged, feel confident knowing that your simple response at least got the other person's wheels spinning.

Successful Introduction to Non-Practitioners

30.   *What are some ways I can introduce a close friend/significant other that believes in God but does not practice it to Catholicism (or Christianity in general) without overwhelming them or turning them off to the faith?*

A .   Because Christianity is so dynamic, it can be overwhelming for people who did not grow up learning about it or practicing it. Furthermore, the Catholic Church, instituted by Jesus Christ Himself, may seem daunting because of its rich history and deeply rooted Tradition. Revealing the faith to others is a patient process. Remember that it is not up to you to convert them! God will use you as an instrument to reveal Himself; take comfort knowing it is ultimately God who is working through your words and actions.

To start these conversations, I think it's helpful to ask people what they already know about Catholicism and what questions they have. This way, you can understand what they already accept, learn what's difficult for them to accept, and find the missing pieces in their understanding.

Furthermore, you won't insult their intelligence by "stating the obvious," thus turning them off to further inquiry. Another aspect to keep in mind is that most people tend to fear conflict, questioning, and change. These three fears can make conversation about religion difficult! All the more reason to be patient through the process.

Practically speaking, I find it beneficial to introduce others to Catholicism by emphasizing that Jesus is at the center. Start by talking about who He is, what He did, and what He continues to do. Emphasize God's desire to be in relationship with His beloved children, and that the Church is a gift, given to us by Jesus – God Himself. The Church helps us grow in relationship with God and understand His will for us. Christian translates to "little Christ," so as Christians, we commit ourselves to imitating Jesus Christ. He is the head, and we, the Church, are His body, living out His will on Earth.

An amazing way to communicate Catholicism is through the transcendentals, or properties of being, beauty, truth, and goodness. Everyone comes to the Church through one of these three aspects. Find which one appeals most to the person to whom you are speaking and speak to how the Catholic Church profoundly exemplifies beauty, truth, or goodness. Each of these properties point to their source, God, and the reality of each of these properties is undeniable. Nobody can stand before something truly beautiful and not be moved to think of its source.

People long to know the truth: to get to the essence of what and why something is. And every human is made "very good," is naturally oriented to the good, and desires goodness in their lives. The Catholic Church is filled with beauty – art, architecture, music, liturgy, lifestyle. The Catholic Church attracts people to the truth – Scripture, the Magisterium, moral guidance. The Catholic Church also attracts people through its goodness, radical service, education, genuine care and the principles of Catholic Social Teaching. If someone is particularly drawn toward one of these transcendentals, show them the way the Catholic Church exemplifies it.

Hypocrisy in the Church

31

31.   *How does one deal with hypocrisy in the Church? Both within the Church and of its members, there is a feeling that it's for "members only" not making much room for the marginalized? When I think of families and couples who are "friends with the pastor" or in well-established friend groups, it makes it difficult to feel welcomed.*

A.   Hypocrisy in the Church is manifested in a multitude of ways, since the Church is composed of human beings who are sinners. It can be difficult to see the Church as the unified Body of Christ when there are certain people within individual parishes who do not have a welcoming disposition. It is important to remember Jesus' words in Matthew 25:40, "And then the king will say to them in reply, 'Amen I say to you, whatever you did for one of these least brothers of mine, you did for me."

Each member of the Body of Christ should know that Jesus emphasizes care and inclusion of the marginalized. As "little Christs," we need to make this a top priority in our

Church and in our larger communities. One of the best ways we can deal with exclusion is to be someone who includes. Instead of waiting to be brought in by a particular group, be the person who brings others in.

There are likely many others who feel excluded as well. Forge your own relationships and be the person who gives off a friendly vibe to everyone, including those who are well-established. Before you know it, bridges will be built and the whole parish family will feel more connected and supported.

Reaching Out to Christians & Non-Christians

32.   *Saint Augustine said: "No man can find salvation outside the Catholic Church." What makes Catholicism the fullness of the truth beyond general Christianity? Should we reach out to other Christians (as well as those who do not know Christ) in evangelization?*

A .   First, let's shed some light on the quote. While St. Augustine said this in the fifth century, the same message has been communicated throughout all of Church history, beginning with Pope St. Clement in his Epistle to the Corinthians in the first century. Phrased positively, "no salvation outside the Catholic Church" means that all salvation comes from Christ the Head through the Church which is His Body. Remember that the Catholic Church, which was instituted by Jesus Christ, was the only Christian Church prior to the Reformation. The sacrament of baptism is an essential for any Christian, and this is a sacrament that has remained tried and true since Jesus instituted it. *Any* Christian baptism really is a Catholic baptism!

We are all baptized into ONE, holy, catholic, and apostolic Church through ONE baptism. Granted, as Christians "protest" certain teachings of the Catholic Church, they are considered Protestants.

When reading St. Augustine's quote since the Reformation, it can seem more exclusive than it really is. During the 1960s, the Second Vatican Council shed some light on its meaning with *Lumen Gentium*. About Christian communities which are not Catholic, the Council declared that they are consecrated through baptism, even if they are not in full communion of belief.

Many Christian Churches even recognize and accept other sacraments as well and are united to the Catholic Church through the Holy Spirit, prayer, and other spiritual benefits. We are all unified as one flock under one shepherd, even if we are not in full unity of belief. Yet, Christ desires for us to be in full union with one another. In St. Paul's letters, we see countless times that he is calling for unity in the Church. This means that we should reach out to people of other Christian denominations, find connections, and strive for a sense of unity that is rooted in Truth.

It is important to note that *Lumen Gentium* also addresses that the plan of salvation includes those who implicitly seek God and strive to do His will as they know it through their conscience. This includes those who, through no fault of their own, have not arrived at an explicit knowledge of God, those who do not know Christ, His Gospel, or His Church, and those who acknowledge the Creator but are not explicitly Christian (the first of whom are Muslims, who hold the faith of Abraham).

God, in His great mercy, does not deny the graces necessary for salvation to these people, for whom whatever good or truth is found amongst them is looked upon by the Church as preparation for the Gospel. Yet it is through Christ's Catholic Church, the universal help towards salvation, that the fullness of the means of salvation can be achieved.

Because of this, we want to share the joy and peace that the Catholic Church can give. This is not done through force, coercion, or manipulation. It is simply done by authentically sharing the Gospel.

This is an obligation imposed on every disciple of Christ, according to his state (*Lumen Gentium*, 21). Christ is the source of salvation for the whole world, and it is through the Church, which is led by the Holy Spirit, that God's plan may be fully realized.

Is It Okay To Befriend Nonbelievers & Non-Catholics?

33.   *Is it okay to make friends with non-believers or people who do not share the same faith?*

A .   Absolutely! It's healthy to have friends from all walks of life so that you can learn from one another and appreciate others' experiences, mentalities, and practices. Life becomes richer when you can dialogue with other people who don't share your faith. It's important to recognize that if you avoid talking about your belief systems, you might find that the relationship is a "surface-level friendship."

Because your faith is so central to your personhood, it can be difficult to grow roots in a friendship in which you do not communicate about it. However, if you can communicate on a philosophical and spiritual realm – even if you have different views – you might find that the friendship is even deeper than friendships in which you do share the same faith! The important thing is that you have people in your life who lift you up and help you call to mind life's deepest realities.

Catholic College Students Are Free to Evangelize

34.   *How can college students begin to care less about what others think of them even in terms of religion?*

A .   As believers, what God thinks of us is most important not what others think. To "care less" of what others thinks takes time because it begins with a deeper relationship with the Lord and prayer. Becoming more forthright with your faith is simply being who you are created to be. Perhaps learn more about the saints, and this will help you to discover a deeper path of goodness and of holiness in day to day life.

Remember always that detaching our hearts from "the world" will draw us closer to God. A deep prayer life, living a sacramental life, practicing the spiritual and corporal works of mercy, and being open to the will of God helps all of us to be closer to Him and "detached" from the world.

Building a Desire for Mass

35. *How can I build a desire to Go to a Mass and practice my faith?*

A.   Your interest in building a desire for going to Mass is exciting, and you are not alone in your pursuit. College is most likely the first time in your life when YOU are in charge of this decision in your life. Do I go to Mass or not?

Up to this point, your parents possibly took you or made you go to church. If you went to a Catholic high school, you might have celebrated Mass during school once a week or once a month, and you had to go.

So, there is a major shift that happens from the feeling of "have to" to "want to" go to Mass. Going to Mass in what feels like the "have to" state in life is an incredibly good thing, even if you feel like you were "forced" to go. It is a good thing because it is showing you that Mass is something your family values and your school knows is important. It also helps create a good habit of going to Mass on Saturday evening or Sunday morning. At the same time, you may not have had a say in whether or not you participated.

Then you go away to college and your parents are not there to wake you up for Mass, or drive you, or walk in with you. Your university does not have a requirement that you must attend. Now, you are fully in the "want to" phase of this reality. It is YOUR decision! There might be internal struggle happening: I know I should go to Mass, but I have been "forced" to for so long, that now that I don't "have to," do I "want to?" How can I make myself "want to" go? This is a major transition that college students face.

In your question you didn't indicate a feeling of being "forced" to go to Mass, however I hope you will allow me to address this experience through this question since it is a quite common experience and reality of college students.

Some suggestions in building the desire to want to go to Mass:

- *Perspective:* I recommend shifting your understanding of your Mass attendance history. Instead of thinking of the last 18+ years of your life as being 'forced' to do something, think of it more as a foundation that was being built for you. Now, with that foundation, you are asked to make your own adult decision about your attendance at Mass.

- *Role:* You have an especially important role in the Mass. In the Constitution for the Sacred Liturgy, the full and active participation of the congregation is to aim to be considered all else. The hope is that Church is helping you feel invited to participate.

The idea behind this is that going to Mass is a lot different from going to a movie. You are not an audience member, but an active participant in the Liturgy. Perhaps when you were a kid you saw people playing a game during recess, and while you enjoyed watching the game, you knew you would have more fun if you participated.

Approach the Mass with that idea in mind. The more actively you participate in the Mass by singing, reciting the prayers, praying during the silence, and acknowledging other people there, the more you can build a desire to attend Mass. You have a part to play!

- *Community:* You are not alone! The communal nature of the Catholic faith is what gives us strength. We are celebrating our faith together.

As a community, each person has a responsibility to care for one another. Is there someone you know who attends Mass regularly? If so, ask to go with them. Going with a friend always aids in feeling connected at Mass.

If you don't know anyone who goes, you might have to be bold and introduce yourself to someone. "Hi, my name is Genevieve. What's your name? Do you usually come to this Mass?" Getting to know the other students who attend Mass and building a community with them is a great way to have a stronger desire to go to Mass. Also, go to Mass early in the semester so you can create a normal routine that fits into your college life.

- *Grace:* The Eucharist is the source and summit of the Catholic faith. God is truly present in the Sacrament. The Eucharist is true food for our souls when we receive Christ in the sacrament. There is much to learn about this gift of our faith by reading the Catechism of the Catholic Church in Part Two "The Celebration of the Christian Mystery." The Catechism tells us that the entire sacramental life of the church points toward the Eucharist. We unite ourselves with Christ and He unites Himself to us in this sacrament. The Eucharist is true bread for our souls.

If you need "proof" that the Eucharist is Jesus and Jesus is who He says He is, I encourage you to google Eucharistic Miracles or visit therealpresence.org.

One reason I am motivated to attend Mass every week without fail is that I am convinced, without a shadow of a doubt that the Eucharist really is the body, blood, soul, and divinity of Jesus.

Consider this: Catholicism is the only religion on the planet that believes that their God is physically present perpetually on the earth with them, and not only does He desire to be worshipped and adored in the tabernacle, but He desires to become one with you in the reception of Holy Communion. If this is true, then why in the world would you ever want to miss an opportunity for the living God to enter your heart – it only will help make everything else better!

- *Adult Responsibility:*   Your parents are not driving you to Mass each Sunday. You are now in the driver's seat. Your decision to go to Mass is one of the many decisions you will be making in college, as an adult.

Acknowledging a healthy sense of obligation and adult responsibility – that you are responsible for your faith formation – is quite empowering!

Keeping Schoolwork and Faith Life in Balance

36. *How does one balance and prioritize schoolwork and faith life?*

A.   How do I find the time!? You already have so many commitments with classes, clubs, athletics, homework, employment. How on earth do you fit faith into your life? St. Francis is quoted as saying, "Let us find God in the midst of so much busyness." How do we do that?

First of all, you must know that the very best way to serve the Lord is to be true to your "state in life." Your state in life includes many roles, such as child, sibling, friend. During your college years, your very specific state in life is college student. Those other roles that you have in your life do not disappear, but most of your time is spent living as a college student. Because that is your main state in life now, that is where you must focus your attention, priorities and responsibilities.

When looking at the big picture of life, God has blessed each of us with two things: my *self* and my *time*. For this question we will focus on the latter: time. Before you can figure out how to balance schoolwork and your faith life, you must first honestly account for your time.

Take a week or two weeks and keep track, either on paper or electronically, *every single thing* you do and how much time you spend doing it. Include everything: sleeping, getting dressed, talking with your roommate, going to class, eating meals, napping, working out, studying, scrolling through social media, watching videos, praying.

Please note, lying to yourself defeats the purpose. You truly want to get a sense of where all your time goes! Once you have an honest picture of your routine, then you can see where there are opportunities for faith development, prayer, and other spiritually enriching experiences.

I have often seen college students who want to be more involved in their faith or want to pray more, jump to do more, when that does not have to be the case. Living your faith in college is not the same as registering for a class. It can and should be lived at *all* times.

With that said, carving out some "you and God" time might be a good idea if your schedule is overwhelming. I advise that you find your God time within your established routine.

For example, saying that you will wake up an hour earlier each day to pray most likely won't work. You already don't wake up that early.

Where are the moments in your day where you can bring in the divine? Brushing your teeth? Walking to class? These could be times of prayer for you. One of my college friends would pray every time he opened a door.

As he left his residence hall, he prayed for a great day. As he entered his classroom, he prayed for his learning. As he walked in the cafeteria, he prayed for his friends and their conversations. Finding time for God within your day is a great way to feel connected to your faith life without having it be one more thing you need to do.

If you noticed in your routine that you actually have more time than you thought, you can consider getting involved in faith centered programs on your campus. What would you like to do? What is going on? I hope that on your campus there are opportunities to gather with other Catholic college students for small groups, service projects and retreats. Be sure to seek out the Newman Center or Campus Ministry department on your campus to see what is available for you to do.

Remember that your state in life is a college student. Your classwork and assignments are your most important time commitments. Be faithful to those while also being honest about how you are spending and dedicating your time. The next question highlights this issue perfectly.

37

Increasing Faith Excitement

37. *What are some ways I can get more excited about my faith?*

A.   Your question reminds me of a section of a prayer by Thomas Merton, "My desire to please You, does in fact please You." The fact that you desire more excitement in your faith life, is worth getting excited about!

Perhaps the loss of excitement is an indication that it is time to shake things up a bit and try something new. Just as we develop and change physically, intellectually and emotionally, we also develop and change spiritually. In college, you are learning more complex subjects, your body is maturing, your social skills are developing. What is your spirituality and prayer life like? Is it the same as it was in middle school?

I can understand why you are not as excited about faith – you are not the same person! I like to think that God presents us with moments of "dryness" so that we can develop our understanding of God and our relationship with God in a new way. It's like God saying, "I want you to know me, understand me, love me in a new, different and deeper way."

Some practical suggestions:

- Think of the most recent time that you really felt connected to your faith. Confirmation? A time at Mass? Talking with your friend or professor about the faith? A certain prayer style? Then reflect on why that was a meaningful moment for you. Why did that create a spark for you? Is it possible to recreate it? I am not suggesting you go back in time and stay there, but to take a moment in your past that was meaningful and see how it can be present in your life today.

  For example, did you experience a connection to your faith during your Confirmation Retreat? If so, you won't be going back to the same retreat, but you can see if there are any religious retreats being offered through Campus Ministry at your college or university.

- What is your passion? I like to think that excitement comes from being and feeling connected. How can your life connect to your faith life? Ultimately the hope is for them to be indistinguishable, and exploring the passions that God has uniquely placed on your heart is a wonderful starting point. What are the things that you ARE excited about? Then explore how the Church celebrates your passion. For example, if you are passionate about helping others by caring for people who are poor or experience homelessness, read about Catholic Social Teaching. If you are passionate about science and the environment, read Pope Francis's document,

Laudato Si – Care for our Common Home. If you are passionate about poetry and art, there is a wealth of Catholic beauty through architecture, paintings, and writings. Not only can you be connected to these elements of faith through knowledge, but also through action. I get excited when learning about things, but I also get excited when I can do something! What service events are being offered at your university? Is there a Club that focuses on Environmental issues? Or opportunities for creative expression? Connect your passion to your faith and then act!

- Talk to others. Excitement about faith can be contagious. Do you know a fellow student who seems excited about their Catholic faith? If you feel comfortable, ask to talk with them. You can also talk with a Catholic campus minister on campus or at the Newman Center.

(There is another question in this book about connecting with people who are like-minded and want to practice their faith. Please see the question and answer on pages 59-60.)

Understanding the Language of Scripture and Prayer

38. *How can I learn to understand the language of Scripture or devotionals? I usually have a difficult time understanding the meaning because of the multiple words, people, or events I don't know about.*

A.   It is exciting to hear that you are interested in diving deeper into Scripture and Catholic devotionals to pray and grow in your faith. It can be quite disheartening and confusing when you don't understand language, time frame, and who people are!

My suggestion is to hone in on a particular topic or book of the Bible where you want to start. What are you interested in learning about? Check out www.usccb.org This is the website for the United States Conference of Catholic Bishops, where you will find many resources on Scripture and prayer. Remember that the Bible isn't a book, it is a library. Select one book on which to focus, then find a companion – either a book, online resource, friend, or study group to help you with a careful study.

The Sermon on the Mount

39.   *In the sermon on the mount, Jesus preaches such high standards of morality. Regarding specifically what He professed about shifting our perspective on justice and fairness to be centered on mercy, particularly about what He said with an eye for an eye and loving our enemies, how do we find the balance of selfless love that is called to serve others with all that we are while preserving and considering our own dignity, well-being, and even sanity?*

A.   The call to serve others is at the heart of the Christian faith and Jesus challenges us to do that in many ways in the Gospel. One of the passages that comes to mind is Matthew 25: 31-45: "When the Son of Man comes in His glory, and all the angels with Him, He will sit upon His glorious throne, and all the nations will be assembled before Him. And He will separate them one from another, as a shepherd separates the sheep from the goats. He will place the sheep on His right and the goats on His left. Then the king will say to those on His right, 'Come, you who are blessed by my Father. Inherit the kingdom prepared for you from the foundation of the world. For I was hungry, and you gave Me food, I was thirsty, and you gave Me drink, a stranger and you welcomed Me, naked and you clothed Me, ill and you cared for Me, in prison and you visited Me.' Then the righteous will answer Him and say, 'Lord, when did we see you hungry and feed you, or thirsty and give you drink?'

And the king will say to them in reply, 'Amen, I say to you, whatever you did for one of these least brothers of mine, you did for Me.' Then He will say to those on His left, 'Depart from me, you accursed, into the eternal fire prepared for the devil and His angels. For I was hungry, and you gave Me no food, I was thirsty, and you gave Me no drink, a stranger and you gave Me no welcome, naked and you gave Me no clothing, ill and in prison, and you did not care for Me.' Then they will answer and say, 'Lord, when did we see you hungry or thirsty or a stranger or naked or ill or in prison, and not minister to your needs?' He will answer them, 'Amen, I say to you, what you did not do for one of these least ones, you did not do for Me.' "

Being selfless – giving of ourselves to others – can be done by helping others meet their basic needs – clothing, food, friendship. Through our selflessness, we honor the dignity of those we are serving. Yet, in that service, we cannot lose sight of our own dignity.

But let's stretch this out a little bit. We know that we are called to serve others in faith. What happens when our kindness and generosity begins to affect us in a negative way?

For example, you might have a friend who is very needy. She wants to talk all the time, or texts you nonstop, with messages that are urgent or depressing which makes you want to help her. Giving your time to your friend is what a faithful person does! But what happens when you are not getting enough sleep, or you are missing assignments because you couldn't get them done in time?

What should you do when you feel that you have been so occupied by her life, that you have neglected your own? It is good to know that creating boundaries that can prevent burnout is 100% okay to do!

This doesn't mean that you don't help or stop caring for your friend, but it allows you to let your friend know that you have limits. Creating boundaries such as time limits, or text limits will help you navigate a relationship that is affecting your life in a negative way.

As a last thought, there is a balance between being selfish and selfless that requires prayer and a good listening ear to the voice of God. Active listening is an art we can practice not only with others but more importantly, with the Lord.

Internalizing Rejoicing in the Lord

40.   *Given the apostolic injunction to rejoice and that we must place our trust in God who promises to prosper us and to give us hope and a future, where is there room for sadness? To what extent is it justified to be upset about the difficulties that we encounter and the internal turmoil we sometimes face? We are still human after all.*

A.   We are indeed called to "Rejoice and Be Glad" as we hear Jesus say in the Beatitudes. Also, Pope Francis tells us the same message in his apostolic exhortation, *Gaudete et exultate*. Why are we called to rejoice and be joyful? We are all called to be saints. That doesn't mean we can't experience anger or fear or sadness – but that the reality of the joy in our lives comes from a much deeper source – from our identity as children of God, called to live our best lives for Him.

Joy is not an external emotion – it is an internal reality; therefore, it is not on the same level as our external emotions – the feelings we experience because of day to day life: anger over being treated rudely, happiness that we got a good grade, sad when a relationship ends. Those emotions are a result from external forces. Yet joy comes from an internal source – the life of God within us. In fact, Joy is a fruit of the Holy Spirit, which means it comes from God's grace within us and not by an external reality.

So, in truth, we are NOT called to be "happy" all the time. That is impossible. We are not called to suppress or hide our emotions. They are a part of us because there are so many things in life – things external to us that affect us. There is a time for every emotion, as we see in the passage from Ecclesiastes 3:

"There is a season for everything, a time for every occupation under heaven: time for giving birth, a time for dying; a time for planting, a time for uprooting what has been planted...
A time for killing, a time for healing;
    a time for knocking down, a time for building.
A time for tears, a time for laughter;
    a time for mourning, a time for dancing.
A time for throwing stones away,
    a time for gathering them;
    a time for embracing,
    a time to refrain from embracing.
A time for searching, a time for losing;
    a time for keeping, a time for discarding.

A time for tearing, a time for sewing;
    a time for keeping silent, a time for speaking.
A time for loving, a time for hating;
    a time for war, a time for peace."

This passage is to remind us that there is time for everything within the seasons of our lives. There will be times of sadness and times of happiness, yet through it all we know God is with us and this gives us joy.

Living a joyful life (rejoicing) and having trust in God, are not the same thing as experiencing emotions like anger or sadness. Rather, emotions and feelings, both positive and negative, can and do have a proper place within a joy-filled and trust-filled life with God.

Being a "Good Person" Is Not Enough

41.   *Why is it not enough to just be a "good person?"*

A.   The word "good" can mean different things in different circumstances. When thought of in a theological context, we see this word in the creation story in Genesis. God declares the world "good" and "very good" thus categorizing His creation in way that signifies its essence, reality and foundational truth. Creation is good in its ontological sense – its design and intent to show God's glory and power. Human beings and creation are inherently good because of our creation!

When the word good is used in an everyday familiar context, such as, "That was a good movie." "The pizza is really good." The word is used in terms of opinion. This is where it gets tricky when we as human beings refer to ourselves as "good" in this familiar way. Anyone can claim to be a "good" person since it could simply be a matter of opinion!

Goodness is a fruit of the Holy Spirit and reflects the nature of God. Goodness relates directly to morality, as virtue in action. So, when we see good actions, we declare the person performing those actions as "good," but it tells us nothing about the person's faith. Catholic teaching tells us that works are a part of and complete the faith.

Relativism is also at play in this question. If I believe I am a good person, then doesn't that make me a good person? We can create our own worlds where we decide how good we are. I often hear the phrase, "as long as you are a good person," but whose opinion are we following for the "good" to *actually be* "good?" Our own? Our mother's? Our society?

Our Catholic faith teaches us that relying on God through our on-going conversion and relationship with Him is even more important since Christ is the eternal "truth" of all we live and believe. The combination of living virtuously and loving God is the best way to live out our faith and therefore also be "good."

Our society says we can decide on our own what is truly "right" from "wrong." If we turn to the Church, we learn that God's truths reveal what is good and bad in His eyes and in the eyes of our Catholic faith.

Being a "good person" in light of making outreach to the marginalized, caring about people in big and small ways and simply living a virtuous life is very important. The problem or confusion arises when we equate goodness with holiness, which is ultimately what we are called to be. Contemplate on how God is calling you to be virtuous in all circumstances. He is always speaking to us through prayer and discernment.

Family Spiritual Politics

42.   What if our parents don't agree with our religion and tend toward a more "politically-based" mentality about life in general? How do we stay true to the faith if we come from a family that truly couldn't care less about religion or faith when all that is discussed or cared about is politics?

A.   Although you may not come from a religious-based family, your faith is your own despite what other family members believe or don't believe. A suggestion may be to connect with other believers and create a support system for you to discuss your faith. As frustrating as it is to come from a family who does not really practice the faith, pray for them. God is with you – even in challenging moments. Don't give up on your prayers for your family.

More From Our Heart

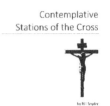

Contemplative Stations of the Cross

Brief, poignant and pocket-sized reflections on the fourteen traditional Stations of the Cross. Published with Ecclesiastical Approval.

$1.99

A Contemplative Las Posadas

An advent devotional featuring themes derived from the traditional Posada Navideña; a Mexican novena that reenacts the journey of St. Joseph and the Blessed Virgin Mary from Nazareth to Bethlehem.

$4.99

Our Radio Show

Young Catholics Respond is a half-hour conversation with inspiring authors, empowering evangelists, knowledgeable theologians and compassionate clergy that help young people to live their Catholic faith boldly. It is available wherever you listen to podcasts.

Made in the USA
Coppell, TX
15 October 2021

64122647R00069